Mrs. Kitty's Cooking Goodness Cookbook

Mrs. Kitty's Cooking Goodness Cookbook

By Carlene Cohen

I will bless the Lord at all times: his praise shall continually be in my mouth.

Psalm 34:1

The Lord is my shepherd, I shall not want. He maketh me to lie down in green pastures: he leadeth me beside the still waters. He restoreth my soul: he leadeth me in the paths of righteousness for his name's sake.

Yea, though I walk through the valley of the shadow of death, I will fear no evil: for thou art with me; thy rod and thy staff they comfort me. Thou preparest a table before me in the presence of mine enemies: thou anointest my head with oil; my cup runneth over. Surely goodness and mercy shall follow me all the days of my life: and I will dwell in the house of the Lord forever.

Psalms 23:1-6

The Lord's Prayer

Our Father, which art in heaven,
Hallowed be thy Name.
Thy Kingdom Come.
Thy will be done in earth,
As it is in heaven.
Give us this day our daily bread.
And forgive us our trespasses,
As we forgive them that trespass against
Us.
And lead us not into temptation,
But deliver us from evil.
For thine is the kingdom,
The power, and the glory,
Forever and ever.
Amen

The Serenity Prayer

God grant me the serenity
to accept the things I cannot
change; courage to change the
things I can; and wisdom to know
the difference.

Living one day at a time;
enjoying one moment at a time;
accepting hardships as the pathway
to peace; taking, as He did, this
sinful world as it is, not as I would
have it; trusting that He will
make all things right if I surrender
to His Will; that I may be reasonably
happy in this life and supremely
happy with Him forever
In the next.
Amen

Meats

Season Mixture for Chicken

What you will need:

2 tbsp garlic salt
2 tbsp chicken base
1 tbsp black pepper
1 tbsp season salt
Container or jar with a lid

Mix all ingredients together. Shake well.

Season Mixture for Pork

What you will need:

2 tbsp garlic salt
1 tbsp black pepper
1 tbsp season salt
½ tbsp salt
Container or jar with a lid

Mix all ingredients together, shaking well.

Southern Style Baked Chicken

What you will need:
1 cut chicken
½ stick of real butter
2 tbsp chicken base
2 cups water
2 tbsp season mixture for chicken
black pepper

Rub chicken parts with season mixture. Cover the chicken and let pieces marinate in the refrigerator for at least 1 hour. Remove chicken and place parts in a large shallow baking dish. Sprinkle black pepper onto the pieces of chicken. Wisk chicken base and 2 cups of water together in a bowl and pour into baking dish. Cover dish and bake for 1 hour at 350 degrees. Remove cover, add water as needed and cook for another 20 minutes. Serves approximately 3 to 4.

Steak and Gravy

What you will need:
4 to 5 pounds of cubed steak
1 cup of flour
1 sliced onion
2 tbsp beef base
2 cups water
Cooking oil of choice

In a deep frying pan, heat cooking oil to 365 degrees. Batter steak pieces with flour and deep fry each piece for 3 to 5 minutes. Remove steak and let it drain on a paper towel. Place steak pieces in a shallow baking dish and cover with sliced onions. In a small bowl, mix 2 tbsp beef base with 2 cups of the water and pour over steak and onions. Cover the steak and bake at 350 degrees for 45 minutes. After 45 minutes. Remove cover and follow gravy recipe on the following page. Serves 3 to 4.

Brown Gravy for Steak and Gravy

What you will need:
2 tbsp beef base
3 tbsp butter
3 tbsp flour
2 cups water

In a saucepan and on low heat, melt butter and slowly add 3 tablespoons of flour while stirring. In a bowl, mix 2 tbsp beef base with 2 cups of water and until beef base dissolves. Pour beef base mixture into saucepan while stirring briskly. Allow ingredients to simmer until thick. Pour the gravy over steak, and cook at 300 degrees for another 15 minutes.

Grilled Pork Chops

What you will need:

4 to 5 pork chops
2 tbsp garlic salt
1 tbsp season salt

In a small bowl, mix garlic salt and season salt together. Rub both sides of pork chops with season and place in refrigerator to marinate for at least 30 minutes. Grill chops on medium heat for 4 to 5 minutes on both sides. If using a frying pan, place a little cooking oil in the pan and fry chops on medium heat for 4 to 5 minutes on each side. Serves 4 to 5 people.

Salmon Cakes

What you will need:

2 can of Salmon
4 eggs
2 chopped small onion
2 tsp flour
4 tbsp bread crumbs
Cooking oil

In a medium bowl, mash salmon, onions, eggs, flour, and bread crumbs together. With your hands, form 7 to 8 salmon patties. In a frying pan, heat a little cooking oil on medium low heat. Fry salmon patties on each side for 3 to 4 minutes. Serves 4 people.

Pot Roast

What you will need:

1 Large Roast
1 large sliced onion
3 tbsp beef base
2 cups water

On a large baking sheet, rub 2 tbsp all over roast, cover and place in refrigerator to marinate for 1 hour or longer. Remove roast and place in a deep roast pan with lid. Place sliced onions over roast and a few in the bottom of the pan. Mix 1 tbsp beef base with 2 cups of water, and pour into roasting pan. Cover roast and bake at 375 degrees for 3 hours. Check water levels throughout baking and add as needed. Remove roast after 3 hours and let stand for 15 minutes. Push a cooking thermometer into the center of the roast and check for a temp of 145 to 155 degrees.

Chili Beans

What you will need:

1 lb of ground beef or ground turkey
½ cup chopped onions
½ cup chopped bell pepper
18 oz of tomatoes sauce
1 can diced tomatoes
2 cans drained kidney beans
2 cans drained pinto beans
1 tbsp salt
2 tbsp chili powder
2 cups water

In a large saucepan, brown ground beef or turkey along with onions and bell pepper on medium heat. Drain any fat remaining on cooked meat and add all remaining ingredients. Cook on medium low heat for 45 minutes. Serves 4 to 5 people.

Meat Loaf

What you will need:

2 lbs ground beef	1 tbsp flour
1 cup oats	1 pack of meat loaf season
2 eggs	
1 small chopped onion	
½ cup chopped bell pepper	
½ cup barbecue sauce	
½ cup ketchup	

In a large bowl, mix all ingredients together. In a loaf baking pan or regular baking pan, shape into a loaf and bake at 325 degrees for 1 hour. Serves 6 to 8 people

Grilled Teriyaki Chicken

What you will need:

5 lbs chicken breast fillet
2 tbsp teriyaki sauce
1 tbsp soy sauce
Cooking oil
Salt

In a medium bowl, mix teriyaki sauce and soy sauce. Season chicken breast will salt and let marinate in refrigerator for 15 minutes. Remove chicken breast and separately dip each piece in sauce mix. In a frying pan, add cooking oil and fry breast on each side for 4 to 5 minutes on medium low heat. If using a grill, eliminate the oil and grill each piece for 4 to 5 minutes on each side. Brush on any remaining sauce while cooking. Serves 4 to 5 people.

Chicken and Dumplings

What you will need:

Chicken	Dumplings
4 skinless chicken breast fillet	2 cups plain flour
2 tbsp chicken base	¼ tsp salt
7 cups water	½ cup cold water

Prepare chicken: Chop chicken breast into cubes or chucks. Boil chicken breast for 15 minutes in 3 cups of water. Cover chicken breast, reduce heat to low heat, and set aside.

Prepare dumplings: Mix flour, salt, and water together until you have a thick dough. Sprinkle a little flour on a flat surface and roll just a bit. Cut the dough into squares and boil in 4 cups of water. While dumplings are boiling, add chicken chunks and chicken base. Reduce heat to a low simmer and let cook for 30 minutes. Serves 4 people.

Baked Ham

What you will need:

1 Whole Ham
½ cup brown sugar
2 cups water,
1 can 7up soda

Place ham in large baking dish and pour 7up soda over ham then rub ham with brown sugar. Pour water into pan and cover with lid or foil. Bake ham at 375 degrees for 2 hours or to a thermometer temperature of 140 degrees.

Beef Stew

What you will need:

2 lbs beef chunks	4 chopped potatoes
1 large chopped onion	2 tbsp beef base
1 can diced tomatoes	garlic salt
2 stalks chopped celery	4 cups water

Add beef chunks, beef base, onions, celery and water. Then cover and boil for 45 minutes on medium heat. Add garlic salt (your desired amount), potatoes and tomatoes. Cook all ingredients for another 15 to 20 minutes on medium low heat. Stir ingredients occasionally. Serves 4 to 5 people.

Chicken Pot Pie

What you will need:

4 boneless chicken breast cut into small chunks
1 pack of frozen mixed vegetables
1 can cream of chicken soup
1 can cream of celery soup
½ cup of the stock from cooked chicken
2 cans pie crust dough or 2 thawed pie crust

Boil chicken chunks with a little salt for 15 minutes. In a separate pot, heat mixed vegetables for about 5 minutes then drain and pour into baking dish. Scoop out chicken and add to vegetables. Add cans of soup and ½ cup of chicken stock. Mix all ingredients together in baking dish. Top mixture with thawed pie crust or dough. Bake at 375 degrees for 25 to 30 minutes. Watch crust periodically to avoid burning. Cover edges of crust with foil during the last 10 minutes of baking if needed. Serves 4 to 5 people.

Irish Beef Stew

What you will need:

2 lbs of beef chunks   dashes of garlic salt
1 large chopped onion   water
1 can diced tomatoes
2 tbsps beef base
2 stalks chopped celery
4 peeled and chopped potatoes

Fill a deep pot halfway with water and add beef, a little garlic salt, onions, celery, and beef base then cook for 20 minutes. Add tomatoes and potatoes cover and simmer on medium low heat for 30 to 45 minutes (until potatoes have cooked down). Let stew sit for 5 minutes on low heat before serving. Serves 4 to 5 people.

Stuffed Green Peppers

What you will need:

5 large bell peppers
½ cup cooked rice
2 lbs ground beef
1 medium minced onion
1 can tomato sauce
1 tbsp Worcestershire sauce

In a saucepan, cook ground beef along with worcestershire sauce and onions. Add tomato sauce (leaving a little to pour over stuffed peppers) and rice then mix all ingredients together. Cup the tops off of each bell pepper and stuff with filling. Add a little water to the bottom of a baking dish and place stuffed peppers in the pan. Bake at 350 degrees for 30 minutes. Pour the remaining tomato sauce over each pepper halfway through baking. Serves 5 people.

Crab Cakes

What you will need:

1 lb of crab meat
1 egg
½ cup of bread crumbs
1 tbsp finely chopped green pepper
1 tbsp finely chopped red pepper
1 tsp dried mustard
2 tsp margarine

In a bowl, mix all ingredients together and form into medium or small crab cakes. Grill or pan fry with margarine on med low heat for about 3 to 4 minutes on each side. Serves 4 to 5 people.

Cabbage Casserole

What you will need:

1 lb ground beef
1 chopped bell pepper
1 chopped onion
1 head of shredded cabbage
1 tsp ketchup
1 tsp tomato sauce
¼ tsp salt
1 bag shredded cheese

Steam cabbage with a dash of salt for 5 minutes on medium low heat and set aside. In a saucepan, cook ground beef, onion, and bell pepper. Drain any fat from ground beef mixture then add tomato sauce and ketchup. Pour steamed cabbage into a casserole dish making sure there is not too much water remaining. Top cabbage with ground beef mixture and shredded cheese. Bake at 350 degrees for 20 minutes. Serves 4 to 5 people.

Grilled Lamb Chops

What you will need:

4 Lamb Chops   black pepper
½ tsp garlic salt   ½ cup soy sauce
3 tbsp cooking oil
½ stick butter
½ cup worcestershire sauce

In a large bowl, add soy sauce, worcestershire sauce, garlic salt, and lamb chops. Using your hands (with gloves if desired) massage or rub each chop with sauce/garlic mix. Cover bowl with plastic wrap and marinate in refrigerator for 8 hours. In a large saucepan, heat oil and butter on med low heat. Add lamb chops and sprinkle black pepper on each chop. Cook on med low heat to desired doneness (for 4 minutes on each side). Serves 4 people.

Cooking is my calling, and I knew this early on in my life. One of the first dishes I prepared with the help of my brother, is macaroni and cheese. Where I am from macaroni and cheese is usually served as a side dish just like green beans, but many people consider it an entree' because of the eggs, cheese, and milk it contains. In my opinion, macaroni and cheese is a very hearty dish and it deserves its own category in cookbooks.

Macaroni and Cheese

What you will need:

16 oz of small to medium shaped pasta
½ cup shredded sharp cheese
½ cup shredded mozzarella cheese
2 eggs
½ cup half n half cream
½ cup sour cream
a little dash

In a medium size pot, bring 2 cups of water to a boil then add pasta and sprinkle in a little salt. Drain pasta and pour into a casserole dish. In a small bowl, add sour cream, 2 eggs, and half and half then whisk into a thick liquid. Sprinkle both cheese over the pasta and then add liquid mixture. Bake at 325 degrees for 30 to 40 minutes. Serves 4 to 5 people.

Vegetables
and
Sides Dishes

Cabbage and Collards

What you will need:

1 head green cabbage
1 bundle of collard greens
A small piece of pork side meat or smoked turkey
1 tsp salt
1 tsp sugar
½ stick of real salted butter
4 cup of water

Wash and chopped or shred cabbage and collard greens. In a medium pot, add all ingredients except cabbage, cover, and cook on medium low heat for 25 minutes. After 25 minutes, add cabbage and cook for 10 more minutes stirring periodically. Serves 4 to 5 people.

Green Beans

What you will need:

1 large can drained green beans
½ stick real salted butter
2 tsp chicken base
2 tsp sugar
½ cup chopped onions
4 cups of water

In a medium pot, add all ingredients and cook on medium low heat for 30 minutes. Serves 4 to 5 people.

Collard Greens

What you will need:

3 lbs of collard greens
A small piece of pork side meat or smoked turkey
1 tsp salt
1 tsp sugar
½ stick of real salted butter
4 cup of water

Wash and chopped collard greens. In a medium pot, add all ingredients, cover, and cook on medium low heat for 45 minutes while stirring periodically. Serves 4 to 5 people.

Turnip Greens and Turnips

What you will need:

3 lbs turnip greens
4 large turnips
A small piece of pork side meat or smoked turkey
1 tsp salt
1 tsp sugar
½ stick of real salted butter
4 cup of water

Wash turnip green leafs and tear into small pieces if desired. Wash and chop turnips into medium/small pieces. In a medium pot, add all ingredients, cover, and cook on medium low heat for 40 minutes while stirring periodically. Serves 4 to 5 people.

Fried Green Tomatoes

What you will need:

4 large green tomatoes
1 egg
1 cup milk
1 tsp salt
1 tsp pepper
2 cups flour
2 cups cooking oil

In a small bowl, whisk egg and milk together. Slice tomatoes into about 3 or 4 slices per tomato. In a small bowl, mix flour, salt, and pepper. In a frying pan, heat cooking oil to 350 degrees or on medium heat. Dip each slice of tomato in the egg wash then batter in flour mixture and carefully place in frying pan. Reduce heat as needed. Cook tomatoes on each side for 3 minutes or until golden brown. Serves 4 to 5 people.

Deviled Eggs

What you will need:

10 hard boiled eggs
¼ tsp salt
2 tsp mayonnaise
1 tsp mustard
½ cup pickle relish

Peel and slice each egg into two then scoop out egg yolk. In a small bowl, mix egg yolk, and all other ingredients until mixture is smooth. Carefully spread yolk mixture into each egg using a spoon or frosting pen. Chill and serve. Serves 4 to 5 people.

Potato Salad

What you will need:

6 large potatoes   ½ tsp sugar
3 eggs   1 tbsp mustard
1 small onion   1 cup pickle relish
2 stalks of celery   1 tsp salt
1 small green or red pepper
1 cup mayo

Peel and dice potatoes then boil for in a little salt for 15 minutes, or until tender. Drain potatoes and let cool in a large bowl while chopping other ingredients. Chop onions, celery, eggs, and pepper then add to potatoes. Add all other ingredients and mix well. Cover potato salad and let chill. Serves 4 to 5 people.

Squash Casserole

What you will need:

6 yellow squash	2 tsp sugar
1 large Vidalia onion	1 tsp salt
1 stick butter	1 tsp flour
1 ½ cup shredded sharp cheese	
½ cup evaporated milk	
1 egg	

Dice and boil squash and onions in a little salt for 10 minutes then drain and pour into casserole dish. Melt stick of butter and pour over squash. In a small bowl, mix egg and flour together then add milk, sugar, and salt. Pour liquid mixture over squash. Stir 1 cup cheese into squash casserole and bake at 350 degrees for 20 minutes. Remove casserole and sprinkle on ½ cup cheese then bake for 10 minutes. Remove and let sit for 5 minutes before serving. Serves 4 to 5 people.

Green Bean Casserole

What you will need:

1 large can fresh cut green beans
1 can cream of mushroom soup
½ stick melted butter
1 can French's crispy fried onions

In a large bowl, mix all ingredients well and pour into a casserole dish. Spread mixture evenly then sprinkle French's crispy fried onions to the top. Bake at 350 degrees for 20 minutes.

Asparagus Casserole

What you will need:

2 can asparagus or 2 lbs of fresh asparagus
½ stick butter
1 can cream of mushroom soup
3 boiled and chopped eggs
4 oz of pimento cheese
1 tube Ritz crackers

If using fresh asparagus, dice each stalk into 1 inch pieces then boil until tender. Add asparagus, pimento cheese, eggs, and cream of mushroom to a casserole dish. Mix all ingredients well and spread evenly over dish. Crumble Ritz crackers and sprinkle over entire casserole. Bake at 350 degrees for 40 minutes. Serves 4 to 5 people.

Broccoli Casserole

What you will need:

2 lbs fresh or frozen broccoli florets
½ stick butter
½ cup chopped onions
½ cup steamed rice
1 box velveeta cheese
½ cup shredded sharp cheese

In a medium pot, boil broccoli florets and onions with a little salt for 15 minutes. Remove from heat and drain most of the water, but leaving some then add velveeta cheese and butter. Add rice to mixture then mix well. Pour mixture into a casserole dish and spread evenly. Sprinkle on shredded cheese and bake at 350 degrees for 40 mins. Serves 4 to 5 people.

Stewed Tomatoes

What you will need:

1 large can diced or whole tomatoes
1 small chopped green pepper
1 small chopped onion
½ stick butter
½ cup sugar
½ cup ketchup
1 cup water
3 slices of bread

In a medium pot, boil all ingredients (except bread) for 25 minutes on medium. Toast bread slices and add to top of tomato mixture then reduce heat to low heat and let stew for 5 more minutes. Stir toast into tomatoes before serving. Serves 4 to 5 people.

Yellow Squash and Onions

6 yellow sliced or diced squash
1 large yellow onion
½ tsp salt
½ tsp black pepper
½ stick of butter
2 tsp oil
1 tbsp sugar
½ cup water

In a medium saucepan, add oil, onions, salt, and pepper then cook on medium heat for 10 minutes. Add squash, sugar, water, and butter. Reduce heat to medium low, cover, and cook for 20 minutes. Serves 4 to 5 people.

Sauteed Zucchini and Yellow Squash

What you will need:

6 sliced zucchini and yellow squash
1 sliced red pepper
1 thinly sliced yellow onion
½ cup chopped scallions
½ stick butter
Hot sauce
Dash of salt

In a medium saucepan, melt butter on medium low heat. Add all ingredients and continuously toss for 7 to 10 minutes or until tender. Serves 4 to 5 people.

Baked Beans

What you will need:

1 large can baked beans
1 tbsp sugar
½ cup brown sugar
½ cup finely chopped onion
½ cup finely chopped green pepper
1 tbsp mustard
2 tbsp Ketchup

In a bowl, mix all ingredients well then pour into a casserole dish. Bake at 375 degrees for 40 minutes.

Baked Beans with Bacon

Follow the previous instructions and add chopped cooked bacon or bacon bits.

Candied Yams

What you will need:

4 large chopped sweet potatoes
½ stick butter
1 cup sugar
½ cup brown sugar
1 tsp nutmeg
1 tsp cinnamon
2 tsp vanilla flavoring

In a medium pot, boil sweet potatoes for 20 minutes then drain most of the water. Pour sweet potatoes into a slightly deep casserole dish and add all other ingredients. Mix ingredients well and then bake at 350 degrees for 20 minutes. Add a little water if need to avoid sticking. Servers 4 to 5 people.

Desserts

Momma's Pie Crust Recipe for Cobblers

What you will need:

3 cups pastry flour
1 tsp salt
½ cup shortening
½ cup very cold butter
½ cup ice water

In a medium bowl, add 2 ½ cup (½ cup of flour will be used during rolling process) of flour then use a pastry cutter or fork and cut cold butter and shortening into flour. When the mixture is crumbly, sprinkle on salt. Add a little water, but not to much and then dump dough onto a flour surfaced. Using your lightly floured hands, knead the dough until pastry forms. Cut dough into 2 pieces, cover with wrap, and chill for 5 minutes. Sprinkle a little flour on rolling pin and flatten dough to about ⅛ inch thick. Carefully place dough on top of cobblers.

If desired, cut a few pieces of dough and place along the sides of cobbler. Another option for cobbler crust, is to purchased your favorite brand of pre-prepared, store bought pastry.

Peach Cobbler

What you will need:

2 large can peaches or 1 bag frozen peaches
½ stick melted butter
1 cup sugar
1 cup water
2 tsp vanilla
1 tsp nutmeg

In a casserole dish, mix all ingredients well and cover the top with Momma's Pie Crust or store bought dough. Bake at 350 degrees for 45 minutes. Keep an eye on crust and reduce heat if it starts to brown too quickly. Serves 4 to 5 people.

Cherry Cobbler

What you will need:

2 cans of cherry pie filling
½ stick melted butter
1 cup sugar
½ cup water
1 tsp vanilla
1 tsp nutmeg

In a casserole dish, mix all ingredients well and cover the top with Momma's Pie Crust or store bought dough. Bake at 350 degrees for 45 minutes. Keep an eye on crust and reduce heat if it starts to brown too quickly. Serves 4 to 5 people.

Blackberry Cobbler

What you will need:

2 cans of blackberries or 1 bag frozen blackberries
½ stick melted butter
1 cup sugar
1 cup water
1 tsp vanilla
1 tsp nutmeg

In a casserole dish, mix all ingredients well and cover the top with Momma's Pie Crust or store bought dough. Bake at 350 degrees for 45 minutes. Keep an eye on crust and reduce heat if it starts to brown too quickly. Serves 4 to 5 people.

Apple Cobbler

What you will need:

2 large can apple pie filling
½ stick melted butter
1 cup sugar
1 cup water
2 tsp vanilla
1 tsp nutmeg

In a casserole dish, mix all ingredients well and cover the top with Momma's Pie Crust or store bought dough. Bake at 350 degrees for 45 minutes. Keep an eye on crust and reduce heat if it starts to brown too quickly. Serves 4 to 5 people.

Strawberry Cobbler

What you will need:

2 lbs fresh or frozen strawberries
½ stick melted butter
1 cup sugar
1 cup water
2 tsp vanilla
1 tsp nutmeg

In a casserole dish, mix all ingredients well and cover the top with Momma's Pie Crust or store bought dough. Bake at 350 degrees for 45 minutes. Keep an eye on crust and reduce heat if it starts to brown too quickly. Serves 4 to 5 people.

Sweet Potato Cobbler

What you will need:

4 large sweet potatoes
½ stick melted butter
1 ½ cup sugar
½ cup brown sugar
2 tsp vanilla
1 tbsp nutmeg

½ can evaporated milk
1 tbsp flour
1 tbsp cinnamon

Topping: Mix together ½ cup brown sugar, 2 tsp flour and ½ cup pecans to make a crumble.

Peel potatoes and cut into large chunks. Boil potatoes for 20 minutes. Remove potatoes from heat, drain some of the water (not too much), and add all other ingredients then mash together. Spoon mixture into a casserole dish. Sprinkle crumble all the over top. Bake at 375 degrees for 30 minutes. Serves 4 to 5 people.

Sweet Potato Pie

What you will need:

4 sweet potatoes

2 eggs

1 stick melted butter

½ cup evaporated milk

1 tsp nutmeg

½ tsp cinnamon

1 ½ tsp vanilla flavoring

1 tsp flour

1 ½ cup sugar

2 frozen pie shells

Peel and boil sweet potatoes then add to a large bowl along with all other ingredients. Mix all ingredients well and pour evenly into pie crusts. Bake at 350 degrees for 45 to 50 minutes or until knife inserted in the center comes out clean. Let pies set for 30 minutes before slicing. Yields 2 pies.

Punch Bowl Cake

What you will need:

1 box yellow cake mix
1 cans drained crushed pineapples
1 can drained cherries
¼ cup chopped pecans
1 or 2 containers of cool whip

Bake cake mix according to package directions for 2 layers and let cool. In a large punch bowl, break cake into pieces and place into bottom of punch bowl. Next spread on cool whip then crushed pineapples and cherries. Keep repeating the layering process until all ingredients are used. Top off with cool whip and sprinkle on pecans. Chill and serve.

Pecan Pie

What you will need:

3 eggs
1 cup sugar
1 cup brown sugar
1 tsp vanilla flavoring
1 stick melted butter
1 ½ cup pecan
2 tsp flour
2 frozen pie crusts

In a bowl, mix all ingredients smoothly (except pecans).
Pour mixture evenly into 2 pie crusts and top with pecans.
Bake at 350 degrees for 45 minutes. Yields 2 pies.

Coconut Pie

What you will need:

1 bag of shredded coconut
3 tbsp flour
1 stick melted butter
1 cup sugar
2 cups buttermilk
3 eggs
1 tsp vanilla flavoring
2 frozen pie shell

In a large bowl, mix sugar and eggs until smooth and then mix in all other ingredients. Pour mixture into 2 pie shells. Bake at 350 degrees for 45 minutes. Yields 2 pies.

Chess Pie

What you will need:

3 eggs
1 cup sugar
1 cup brown sugar
1 tsp vanilla flavoring
1 stick melted butter
2 tsp flour
2 frozen pie shells

In a bowl, mix all ingredients smoothly then pour mixture evenly into 2 pie crusts. Bake at 350 degrees for 45 minutes. Yields 2 pies.

Egg Custard Pie

What you will need:

1 cup sugar
1 tsp flour
1 stick melted butter
2 cups buttermilk
3 eggs
1 tsp vanilla flavoring
2 frozen pie shells

In a large bowl, mix butter, sugar, flour, flavoring, and eggs until smooth.Mix in buttermilk and then pour into 2 pie shells. Bake at 350 degrees for 40 minutes then remove and sprinkle with nutmeg. Yields 2 pies.

Lemon Chess Pie

What you will need:

3 cups sugar
1 tbsp flour
1 stick melted butter
1 tbsp vanilla flavoring
2 large lemons
2 eggs
2 frozen pie shells

In a large bowl, mix all ingredients well (except lemon juice). Add lemon juice and mix well then pour into 2 pie shells. Bake at 350 degrees for 45 minutes. Yields 2 pies.

German Chocolate Pie

What you will need:

1 cup sugar
1 tbsp flour
2 tbsp dark cocoa
1 stick melted butter
1 cup shredded coconut
1 cup pecans

1 tsp vanilla flavoring
3 eggs
1 cup brown sugar
2 frozen pie shells

In a large bowl, blend both sugars, flour, and butter. Add eggs, vanilla, butter, and cocoa then blend until smooth. Pour mixture into pie shells. In a small bowl, mix coconut and pecans then sprinkle over pie filling. Bake at 350 degrees for 40 minutes or until pie looks puffy. Let cool for several hours before slicing. Yields 2 pies.

Rice Pudding

What you will need:

1 lb white rice	2 eggs
3 tbsp raisins	1 tsp nutmeg
½ can evaporated milk	½ stick butter
1 cup sugar	
1 tsp flour	
1 tsp vanilla flavoring	

Steam rice and set aside. Mix all other ingredients together and fold into rice with a fork. Bake at 375 degrees for 40 minutes. Serve hot or cold. Serves 4 to 5 people.

Corn Pudding

What you will need:

1 can whole kernel corn
1 can cream style corn
¼ cup sugar
½ stick margarine
2 tbsp flour
1 cup can milk
2 eggs
½ tsp salt

In a medium bowl, whisk together eggs, milk and flour. In a casserole dish, add all other ingredients then fold in egg mixture with a fork. Bake at 350 degrees for 30 minutes. Serves 4 to 5 people. Corn Pudding can also be served as a side dish.

Blueberry Salad

What you will need:

1 box blueberry jello
1 20 oz can blueberries
1 20 oz can crushed drained pineapples
8 oz box cream cheese
1 cup sour cream
½ cup sugar
½ cup chopped walnuts

Follow instructions in gelatin pack and then stir in blueberries and pineapples. Pour mixture into a casserole dish and chill in refrigerator until firm. While jello is setting, blend together cream cheese, sour cream, and sugar. Once jello has set, evenly spread on creamy mixture and sprinkle with walnuts. Cover with casserole top or plastic wrap and chill overnight. Serves 4 to 5 people.

Carrot Cake

What you will need:

3 cups all purpose flour	1 tsp nutmeg
5 eggs	1 tsp cinnamon
1 ½ cup oil	1 pack walnuts
16 oz can crushed pineapples	
2 ½ cup sugar	½ tsp salt
1 ½ tsp baking soda	1 can spray oil
2 tsp baking powder	
2 tsp vanilla flavoring	
2 cups grated carrots	
1 16 oz container cream cheese frosting	

Preheat oven to 350 degrees. Spray tube cake pan or bundt cake pans or line with parchment paper and set aside. In a large bowl, blend sugar and oil until smooth. Slowly add eggs one at a time and blend until smooth. In a separate bowl, mix all other dry ingredients together and then blend with wet mixture.

Stir in carrots and walnuts and pour batter into cake pan. Bake for 1 hour or until toothpick inserted into center comes out clean. Let cool for in pan for 20 minutes then remove onto a cooling rack and apply frosting.

Pound Cake

What you will need:

2 cups all purpose flour
2 cups sugar
6 eggs
1 cup softened butter
2 tsp vanilla flavoring
1 cup crisco
Dash of salt
1 cup milk

In a large bowl, blend crisco and butter together for 1 to 2 minutes on low speed. Add sugar and blend for 1 minute. Add eggs and vanilla then blend for 1 minute. Add flour and dash of salt then blend for 30 seconds then blend in milk until smooth. Pour mixture into an oil and lightly floured 10 inch tube pan. Bake at 350 degrees for 1 hour 15 minutes. Let cool before removing to wire rack.

Pineapple Upside-down Cake

What you will need:

1 Pack Duncan Hines cake mix
3 eggs
½ cup sugar
1 (4 oz) can crushed pineapples
1 cup packed brown sugar
½ cup butter
⅓ cup oil
1 cup water

Preheat oven to 350 degrees. Follow Duncan Hines cake mix instructions and sit mixture to the side. In a medium bowl, sugar, pineapples, and brown sugar together. Oil the bottom and sides of 9 inch square baking pan, then melt butter inside the pan by placing the pan in preheat oven. Remove pan and spread pineapple mixture along the bottom. Evenly pour cake mixture over pineapple mixture and bake for 45 to 50 minutes or until toothpick inserted in center comes out clean. Immediately after removing from oven, place heatproof serving dish upside down over cake and then flip pan over. Leave pan over the cake for 5 minutes then slowly lift off cake. Serve warm.

Watergate Salad

What you will need:

1 pkg Pistachio instant pudding mix
1 20 oz can crushed pineapples in juice
½ cup chopped pecans
1 ½ cup cool whip
1 ½ cup mini marshmallows

In a bowl, mix instant pudding mix, pineapples, and cool whip. Make sure no dry pudding mix is remaining in the bottom of bowl. Add marshmallows and stir a little more. Sprinkle on pecans and chill. Watergate salad can also be served as a side dish.

Fruit Salad

What you will need:

1 large can chunk pineapples
1 can mandarin oranges
1 cup seedless grapes
2 unpeeled apples cut in cubes
1 cup raisins
1 cup mayonnaise
1 cup pecans

Drain all cans of fruit and pour into a large bowl. Mix fruit with mayonnaise and pecans. Chill and serve. Fruit salad can also be served as a side dish.

Starters
Salads
Soups
&
Breads

Fried Dill Pickles

What you will need:

1 jar sliced dill pickles
1 egg
1 cup milk
4 cups all-purpose flour
¾ tsp salt
½ tsp black pepper
1 quart cooking oil

In a bowl, mix ½ tsp flour, egg and milk together. In a separate bowl, mix 3 ½ cup flour, salt, and black pepper. Heat cooking oil to 375 degrees then individually dip each pickle in egg wash then flour and carefully place in deep fryer. Avoid overcrowding deep fryer with pickles. Fish pickles out of deep fryer once they are golden brown. Drain pickles on a paper towel. Fried dill pickles can also be served as a side dish.

Meatballs

What you will need:

1 lb ground beef	2 stalks chopped celery
1 egg	1 can diced tomatoes
2 tsp worcestershire sauce	½ cup barbecue sauce
2 tsp ketchup	
2 tsp of flour	
½ chopped onion	
1 cup water	

In a medium bowl, beef, eggs, onion, worcestershire sauce, ketchup, and flour together then scoop smalls amounts and roll into meatballs. In a lightly oiled saucepan, brown the meatballs on low heat. Add 1 water, can diced tomatoes, celery, and barbecue sauce and simmer on low heat for 30 minutes. Serve meatballs in a shallow serving dish with long toothpicks. Meatballs can also be served as an entree'.

Chicken Salad

What you will need:

3 boiled chicken fillet breast
6 boiled eggs
1 finely chopped red pepper
2 stalks chopped celery
½ cup mayonnaise
½ cup pickle radish
2 tsp sugar
1 tsp salt
1 ½ tsp mustard

Chop chicken breast into chunks then place in a medium bowl. Chop eggs and add to chicken chunks. Add all other ingredients and mix well. Chill salad and serve on crackers, mini pastry pockets, or sliced baguettes.

Shrimp Salad

What you will need:

2 cups cooked small shrimp
1 cup finely chopped celery
1 ½ cup finely chopped green and red pepper
1 tbsp lemon juice
4 tbsp mayonnaise
½ tsp salt
½ tsp pepper

In a medium bowl, mix all ingredients together and chill for 1 hour. Serve on crackers, mini pastry pockets, or mini baguettes.

Macaroni Salad

What you will need:

½ lb dry macaroni pasta
1 cup pickle relish
3 stalks finely chopped celery
1 finely chopped green pepper
1 cup mayonnaise
1 tbsp red pimientos
1 tsp salt
1 tsp sugar
½ tsp vinegar
1 tsp mustard

In a medium pot, bowl macaroni pasta then drain and add to a bowl. Add all other ingredients and mix well. Chill for 1 hour and then serve.

Cucumber Salad

What you will need:

3 diced cucumbers (peeled or unpeeled)
1 small chopped or sliced red onion
½ tsp sugar
1 ½ cup oil and vinegar salad dressing
½ chopped or sliced sweet onion
Dashes of salt

Place chopped cucumbers in a bowl and dash on salt. Allow cucumbers to sweat in salt for about 30 minutes then drain excess liquid. Add all other ingredients and toss with tongs. Serve immediately or chill before serving.

Potato Soup

What you will need:

4 chopped russet potatoes
1 large chopped onion
1 ½ cup milk
½ stick of butter
1 small can evaporated milk
2 tsp cornstarch
2 cups water

In a soup pot, add potatoes and boil for 10 minutes. Add onions, milks, and butter then cook on medium low heat for 40 minutes. Dissolve cornstarch in a little water then slowly stir into soup while constantly stirring. Reduce heat to low and soup thicken. Serves 4 to 5 people.

Cole Slaw

What you will need:

1 large green shredded cabbage
½ cup shredded carrots
1 cup pickle relish
½ tsp salt
1 tbsp sugar
½ cup mayonnaise

In a bowl, add cabbage and sprinkle on salt. Let cabbage sweat for 30 minutes then drain excess liquid. Add all other ingredients and mix well. Chill for 30 minutes or serve immediately.

Homemade Ranch Dressing

What you will need:

1 pack of Hidden Valley Ranch dressing mix
2 cups mayonnaise
2 cups buttermilk
8 oz of sour cream

In a mason jar or bowl, mix all ingredients together then chill overnight.

French Toast

What you will need:

Bread slices of choice
2 eggs
1 cup milk
½ stick butter
Powdered sugar
Dash salt

In a small bowl, whisk eggs and milk together with a dash of salt. In a frying pan or on a grill, melt butter on medium low heat then dip slices of bread in egg wash coating each side then placing them in pan or on grill. Let brown for 2 to 3 minutes on each side. Remove and sprinkle each piece with powdered sugar. Top with maple syrup, honey, or agave syrup if desired.

Buttermilk Biscuits

What you will need:

4 cups self-rising flour
1 cup shortening
1 ½ cup buttermilk
½ tbsp baking powder
½ tsp salt

Sift flour, baking powder, and salt then add shortening and mix well with hands. Add buttermilk and knead all ingredients together until batter forms. Sprinkle a little flour on a flat surface then add batter. Knead batter 5 to 6 times by folding and turning (repeat folding and turning). With a flat hands, pat dough out until it is about ½ inch thick. Fold the dough and repeat flattening out with flat hand. Use a biscuit cutter and cut dough then place dough on cookie sheet and bake at 400 degrees until golden brown. Melt a little more butter and brush tops of biscuits.

Hush Puppies

What you will need:

2 cups self-rising cornmeal
2 tsp sugar
½ cup self-rising flour
½ tsp salt
1 tsp baking powder
1 cup buttermilk
1 cup finely chopped onions
Cooking oil

In a medium bowl, combine all ingredients except cooking oil. Heat cooking oil to 375 degrees then with small scooper, carefully scoop batter and drop into oil. Cook until golden brown while constantly flipping hushpuppies. Remove and let oil drain on paper towel.

Cornbread

What you will need:

2 cups self-rising cornmeal
1 cup self-rising flour
1 cup cooking oil
2 cup buttermilk
1 egg
2 tbsp sugar

In a medium bowl, mix all ingredients together until smooth. Heat oven to 350 degrees. Pour a little oil into to baking pan or muffin pan before pouring batter into pan. Bake for 25 minutes.

Cornbread Dressing

What you will need:

2 cups of cornbread batter from cornbread recipe
½ cup oil
4 stalks finely chopped celery
1 large chopped onion
2 tsp chicken base
1 tsp pepper
2 tsp poultry seasoning
2 tsp sage
1 box Poultry Mix Stuffing
1 cup water

Preheat oven to 350 degrees then oil baking pan and bake 2 cups of cornbread batter for 20 minutes. In a saucepan, add ½ cup water, celery, and onions then saute' for 10 minutes on medium low heat. Add chicken base, sage, and poultry seasoning then stir. Remove cornbread and spoon into a bowl then add steamed vegetables, pepper, and box of poultry stuffing pack. Add ½ cup water and mix well. Spread mixture into a lightly oiled baking ban and bake for 45 minutes.